THE LOOPING EVALUATION BOOK

Char Forsten, Jim Grant, and Irv Richardson

Printed in the United States of America

Published by Crystal Springs Books
Ten Sharon Road
P.O. Box 500
Peterborough, NH 03458
1-800-321-0401
FAX: 1-800-337-9929

Publisher Cataloging-in-Publication Data

Forsten, Char, 1948-
   The looping evaluation book / written by Char Forsten,
Jim Grant, and Irv Richardson.—1st. ed.
[86] p. : ill. ; cm.
Includes bibliographical references.
Summary : Designed to help teachers and administrators
explore, implement, and evaluate looping programs.
Includes sections on exploring, implementing, evaluating
and support pages. The book consists mostly of
reproducible checklists.
 ISBN 1-884548-29-6
1. Learning—Study and teaching. 2. Teaching. 3. Nongraded
schools. I. Grant, Jim, 1942- . II. Richardson, Irv, 1956- . III.
Title.
371.3–dc21   1999   CIP
LC 99-074299

Editor: Cathy Kingery
Cover and Text Design: Susan Dunholter
Publishing Manager: Lorraine Walker
Spanish Translations by: Miriam Lockhart and Patricia Wheeler

The Looping Evaluation Book

Written by:

Char Forsten
Jim Grant
Irv Richardson

"I wish she was smart enough to teach second grade, too, next year."

— William Goumas, first-grade student
(writing about his first-grade teacher)

Published by
Crystal Springs Books · Peterborough, New Hampshire
1-800-321-0401

Acknowledgments

We acknowledge with thanks:

All the looping educators and students who shared their own experiences and encouraged us to write this book;

Superintendent Ted Thibideau and the staff at Attleboro School District for so generously sharing their knowledge and experiences in their implementation of looping in grades one through eight;

Jay LaRoche, Lorraine Walker, and Christine Landry for their ongoing support and skills in publishing books that make a difference for educators;

Susan Dunholter for her creative gift to bridge a book design with its text;

and to Cathy Kingery, our extraordinary editor, who treated this manuscript like a dear friend.

Dedications

We warmly dedicate this book to the schools where we were teaching principals and where we learned (almost) everything we know and love about multiyear:

Dublin Consolidated School
Dublin, New Hampshire
—*Char Forsten*

Temple Elementary School
Temple, New Hampshire
—*Jim Grant*

Mast Landing School
Freeport, Maine
—*Irv Richardson*

Contents

Preface: What Constitutes a Successful Evaluation Process?

About This Book

How to Use This Book

Part One: Exploring Looping Configurations

Part Two: Implementing Looping Configurations

Part Three: Evaluating Looping Configurations

Part Four: Support Pages

Preface

What Constitutes a Successful Evaluation Process?

"The only thing that endures over time is the law of the farm: I must prepare the ground, put in the seed, cultivate it, weed it, water it, then gradually nurture growth and development to full maturity."
—Steven Covey (1990)

In the above quotation, Steven Covey captures the essence of a successful evaluation process. As former teaching principals of schools with multiyear classrooms, we are committed to helping other educators do with their programs what Covey so eloquently states about the law of a farm: develop an ongoing plan to effectively explore, implement, and assess their looping or multiage classrooms.

The exploration and implementation steps are critical, formative components, and prior to starting a looping classroom, an understanding of both its philosophy and essential components is crucial. Once — or if — looping classrooms are in place, an ongoing assessment or evaluation plan (the summative component) becomes critical. You continually need to evaluate progress toward your goals in order to measure, report, and use your results for improvement of your looping practices. To extend the metaphor of the farm: You cannot just expect looping classrooms to take root, grow strong, and bloom if you do not "cultivate, weed, water," and constantly evaluate their progress.

The results of your evaluation process should not only help you determine the effectiveness of your looping classrooms, but they should also help you identify the areas that need attention or revision. What we also find exciting is that this comprehensive evaluation procedure allows original stakeholders and newcomers alike the benefit of working through the formative steps and becoming active participants in the ongoing assessment. This process will aid even the most experienced looping educators in their ability to validate what they are doing well and to determine possible changes that will make their programs more effective. For example, a teacher discovers after reading one of the parent surveys that a parent might understand their child's academic standing, but not necessarily comprehend how summer learning can bridge the two years. This information, in addition to other discoveries, is vital and can now be used to strengthen the parent-education component of that teacher's looping classroom.

As you read the introduction and checklists, bear in mind that it is not our intention to imply that you will succeed only if you follow our directions. Although each checklist represents what numerous experienced looping educators consider important for effective implementation, use the blank lines at the bottom of each checklist to customize this book to your own configuration.

It is also not our intention to use this book to evaluate teachers. The checklists will help identify the skills and support teachers need, but they are not meant to evaluate teachers' effectiveness in the classroom.

The authors wish you well in the exploration, implementation, and evaluation of your looping classrooms.

This process will aid even the most experienced looping educators in their ability to validate what they are doing well and to determine possible changes that will make their programs more effective.

About This Book

What is looping?

Looping is an instructional design where students progress to the next grade level with the same teacher(s) for two or more years. A looping configuration creates an environment that allows teachers to continuously track student progress over a two-or-more-year time period, and where relationships improve among all involved: students, teachers, and parents. Improved student attitudes and quality academic instruction and learning are at the core of looping classrooms. In a looping configuration, the first day of the second year is more accurately described as the 181st day in a multiyear classroom. Summer activities bridge the two years and are used by teachers and students to reinforce past learning and create new mindsets for the next year's curriculum.

There are numerous forms of looping configurations being used in today's schools. The authors have worked with two-year, three-year, interbuilding, half-day K, and the "school-within-a-school" and modified looping designs. We have found the greatest number of looping classrooms to be created by two teachers from consecutive grades who form a partnership and loop within a school. Not all teachers within a school need to loop. In most cases, only part of a school is looping, because this instructional design works well within a conventional, single-year, single-grade school.

Many, if not most, looping classrooms are heterogeneous. To teach this wide range of learners, teachers learn how to create and use flexible groups for specific instructional purposes — the goal is not to cover curriculum, but to build independent learners who can achieve their personal best. Educators who practice looping seek to maximize learning through more efficient use of their time and through sound teaching practices.

Does looping involve complex change?

Looping is a straightforward concept, a low-risk reform. Any kind of change, no matter how small it might seem, can have a great impact on everything and everyone affected by it. For this reason, it is critical to remember that change is a process, not an event. Educators cannot just implement looping one day and expect to come in the next and find the philosophy understood and the practices working smoothly. One must first understand the philosophy and mechanics of looping, have the will and skill to implement the necessary changes, and be able to recognize and use the reconfigured time to its greatest capacity. It must matter to the teacher before the teacher can make it matter to others. Evaluating your steps toward looping and building in the necessary flexibility will help ensure greater success for all involved.

Why is there so much interest in looping classrooms?

Today's educational standards demand much from both teachers and students, and educators are increasingly confronted with the "quality v. quantity" debate. In looping and multiage configurations, quality outweighs quantity in that it allows teachers more learning time with students in a real-world setting. Perhaps the most important and most satisfying benefit of looping classrooms, however, is the long-term relationships that teachers, students, and their families develop to better meet the needs of individual learners.

With multiage, at least two grades are blended into one classroom over multiple years. Looping is especially appealing to educators because it generally involves a single grade staying together with the same teacher or team of teachers for two or more years. In this age of grade-specific curriculum and testing, looping teachers have the advantage of multiple-year teaching windows to build relationships and gain effective instructional time, while at the same time needing to teach only a single grade of learners at once.

How does *The Looping Evaluation Book* differ from other books on looping practices?

Numerous requests have been made for a comprehensive book that evaluates looping and multiage classrooms. *The Looping Evaluation Book*, like its companion publication, *The Multiage Evaluation Book*, is designed to help you assess and evaluate each step you take toward implementation of multiyear classrooms, from the formative to the evaluative stages. These are the first books to provide a sequential, hands-on, step-by-step approach, written to help you identify and consider all the factors that will eventually lead to a healthy, thriving looping or multiage classroom. Special features include:

- Checklists
- Support Pages
- Rationale behind the chosen process
- Prescribed goals
- Individual/team goals
- Possible consequences of skipping a step
- Space to write the current principal's name
- Sources you have used in your process
- Space to write your plan
- Space for notes or comments for future reference

Why is evaluation critical to success?

How will you know if your looping classroom is working if you do not evaluate its progress? How will you bring on-board new staff members and stakeholders? What will you say if someone asks you to quantify the success of your looping classroom? How will you improve your existing practices and revise them when needed? What staff development, training, and resources are needed for continued success? Answers to these and other questions can be established through an effective evaluation process. A thorough procedure is critical to success when it helps you understand why you are pursuing specific goals, how you might best achieve them, and, finally, how to monitor, report, and use your results for continual improvement.

How will this book help you evaluate your looping classroom(s)?

Are you currently exploring a looping configuration? Are you already implementing this instructional design and attempting to improve, troubleshoot, or evaluate its effectiveness? Are you ready to expand its use in your school or district, but need a process to bring new stakeholders on-board?

This hands-on book is designed to help you look ahead at what needs to be done and to record your steps and experiences throughout your evaluation process. As such, both the past and the future are considered in today's decision-making process. This book will guide you step-by-step along your looping journey. It provides ample opportunities for you to consider, plan, evaluate, and record your reflections and experiences. Too often the history behind an individual school's reform effort is lost when the stakeholders retire or leave the system. This guide will help keep your information organized, and, if the original stakeholders should leave, it ensures that your process has been preserved for future reference.

Who should use this book?

- Individual teachers, principals, and other educators
- Study groups
- Teacher teams

How to Use This Book

Physical Layout

There are four parts to this book. The first three share a consistent format and include a series of checklists and charts for participating educators to complete. The fourth part contains sample reproducible forms, letters, questionnaires, and surveys, ready for revision or immediate use. This final section also provides recommended resources where you can locate further information on specific looping topics.

The four parts are:

    Part One: Exploring Looping Configurations
    Part Two: Implementing Looping Configurations
    Part Three: Evaluating Looping Configurations
    Part Four: Support Pages

Write or Photocopy?

This book can be used in different ways, depending on your own unique situation. Below are two suggestions.

1. Write directly in the book as you work through the evaluation process. This method is effective if you are working individually or as part of a two-or-more-person team. If a large number of teachers will be part of the evaluation process, it might be most effective for each individual teacher to have his or her own copy of the book. (Multiple copies are available at a discount.) This option might be more efficient than photocopying and collating all the checklists and charts for a large number of teachers.

2. Photocopy and collate the checklists, charts, and activities for teachers or study-team members (from one school only) to use. For this scenario, we recommend that a principal or team leader photocopy and collate the checklists and charts in Parts One and Two of the book to give to teachers and/or other members of the study group for their response. Part Three, "Evaluating Looping Configurations," can be used or photocopied by the principal or team leader to record and assess the results for the entire group.

Getting Started

The Looping Evaluation Book is a workbook that can be consumed by individual teachers or photocopied for use by study groups or multiple classrooms in the same school. Decide which of the methods described above is appropriate for you.

These wide margins are great spaces for taking notes!

Next, consider your reasons for completing this evaluation process. Take some time to read through the entire book. If none of the suggested circumstances fits, write your own in the spaces provided. For example:

I/We:

- are investigating looping classrooms and would like to follow a logical process.

- will be implementing looping classrooms and want to take appropriate steps toward success.

- are currently implementing looping classrooms and are troubleshooting to determine the source(s) of our problems and how we might address them.

- are currently implementing looping classrooms and want to develop an ongoing evaluation process that will allow for continual training and improvement.

- Additional reasons:

_____

_____

_____

Each checklist has space for the user(s) to record his/her name, position, and date.

CHECKLIST 1: ✔

Why Looping?

Person(s) responding to this checklist:
Name(s): *Lee Burwell*   *Elizabeth Quinn*
Position: *3rd grade teacher*   *2nd grade teacher*

Name of principal at time of exploration:
I. Richardson   Date: *9/25/98*

EXPLORING

Rationale:

Why adopt looping configurations? This is perhaps the most important question you should ask yourself prior to planning and implementation. You must understand and be comfortable with the philosophy before you can effectively teach in a looping classroom. Once you determine the rationale for adoption, you can then create an evaluation plan that helps you review how it is working. Investigating looping practices is not only the first step in an effective change process, but also a crucial step toward ultimate success. The stakeholders should understand looping practices and then receive appropriate training and support.

Each rationale helps you understand why the checklist is important.

Goals:

- Understand the vocabulary, philosophy, and instructional practices associated with looping classrooms

- Identify the benefits attributed to looping classrooms

The goals serve as a compass to keep you on course.

Additional Goals:

To better understand how the summer can be used to bridge the two years

_____

_____

What can happen when you don't complete a critical step. This helps users be proactive.

Possible Unintended Consequences of Not Doing This Step:

If this step of exploration is bypassed, stakeholders may lack philosophical grounding and skills necessary to create a looping classroom. Remember, both will and skill are the essential ingredients for success.

CHECKLIST 1: ✔

Why Looping?

Directions: Examine and respond to the statements in the following checklist. Check appropriate responses and use the key at the bottom of this page to help you decide which column best reflects your current situation.

I/We understand:	Yes	Some	No	Refer to Support Pages:
1) the research and vocabulary associated with looping practices and know the important differences among looping, multiage, and single-grade classrooms.	✓ EQ	✓ LB		62-63 77-85
2) the advantages (benefits) and disadvantages associated with looping practices and how they pertain to my/our own setting.	✓ EQ	✓ LB		77-86
3) effective management and instructional strategies used in looping classrooms.	✓ EQ	✓ LB		79-85, 86
4) the role of themes and centers in numerous looping classrooms.	✓ EQ	✓ LB		79-85, 86
5) the importance of using flexible grouping strategies.	✓			62, 79-85, 86
6) how summer-bridge activities are effective components of looping classrooms.		✓		62, 79-85, 86
Additional statements of understanding are:				
7) how to prepare students for the summer bridge.				
8)				

KEY:

☐ **Great!** You have a working knowledge of looping practices. Proceed to Checklist 2.

▨ **Further study is strongly recommended.** See Support Pages for suggestions.

▨ **Further study is necessary.** See Support Pages for suggestions.

4 | THE **LOOPING** EVALUATION BOOK

Each checklist has statements for your consideration that help you determine your level of preparedness.

Support pages guide you to helpful resources.

The key helps you determine if you need further study.

CHECKLIST 1: ✓   How Did You Learn About Looping Classrooms?

Directions: Identify the sources for your exploration step in the chart below.

EXPLORING

Books, Research, Articles, and Studies:	School/Classroom Visitations:	"Chatrooms" Web Site/Interview:	Conferences, Seminars, In-Service Workshops:	Audiotapes, Videos, Other:
Looping Q & A	Carol Jones + Sam Walton, 2nd–3rd Loop, Clark Elem.		How Looping Works	The Looping Video
Looping Q + A	Scheduled for 10/12, 8:00 a.m.	Interview: Carol Jones, Clark Elem.	"	
		Teachnet.com	"	
			"	
			"	
Multiyear Lesson Plan Book; Summer Bridge Activities 2nd–3rd Grade		Interview: Carol Jones, Clark Elementary	"	
	(arrow)		"	

Charts provide space to record your findings or action plans.

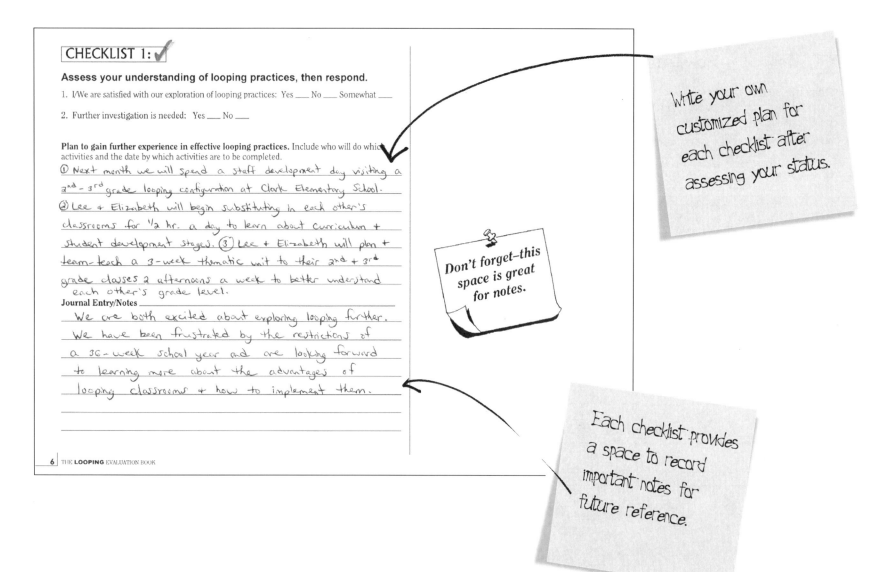

CHECKLIST 1: ✔

Assess your understanding of looping practices, then respond.

1. I/We are satisfied with our exploration of looping practices: Yes ___ No ___ Somewhat ___

2. Further investigation is needed: Yes ___ No ___

Plan to gain further experience in effective looping practices. Include who will do which activities and the date by which activities are to be completed.

① Next month we will spend a staff development day visiting a 2nd–3rd grade looping configuration at Clark Elementary School. ② Lee + Elizabeth will begin substituting in each other's classrooms for ½ hr. a day to learn about curriculum + student development stages. ③ Lee + Elizabeth will plan + team-teach a 3-week thematic unit to their 2nd + 3rd grade classes 2 afternoons a week to better understand each other's grade level.

Journal Entry/Notes

We are both excited about exploring looping further. We have been frustrated by the restrictions of a 36-week school year and are looking forward to learning more about the advantages of looping classrooms + how to implement them.

Write your own customized plan for each checklist after assessing your status.

Don't forget—this space is great for notes.

Each checklist provides a space to record important notes for future reference.

PART ONE: EXPLORING LOOPING CONFIGURATIONS

Checklist ✓ 1. Why Looping? Understanding Looping Philosophy

Checklist ✓ 2. Is a Looping Classroom Right for You?

Checklist ✓ 3. Exploring Different Looping Configurations

EXPLORING

"To what end? . . . is always a good question to ask before the start of any major project."

Exploring looping configurations is the first step toward its effective implementation. Both will and skill are necessary ingredients for success. Too often, we address only the skills needed by educators and avoid or forget that it must matter to us before we can make it matter to others. As Abraham Lincoln said, "Will springs from the two elements of moral sense and self-interest." Whether you are just beginning your exploration of looping or you are troubleshooting or refining your own classroom, the exploration stage should help you understand what looping is and isn't, the reasons for its implementation, and the kinds of instructional practices commonly associated with it.

Directions for Part One:

1. Review the checklists and activities. If you are an experienced looping educator, this is still an important exercise to include in your overall evaluation process.

2. Next, fill in the names and roles of persons completing each checklist.

3. Read the rationale, goal statements, and consequences behind each checklist. Add any additional goals of your own. Goals should be realistic and attainable.

4. Complete the checklists and activities to assess your current situation.

5. Evaluate your readiness (or effectiveness, if already implementing looping) for this step toward creating a successful looping classroom.

6. If needed, create a plan for further exploration. The Support Pages (pp. 60–86) at the end of this book are included to direct you to helpful information.

Refer to "How to Use This Book" (p. xvi) for a completed sample checklist.

CHECKLIST 1: ✔

Why Looping?

Person(s) responding to this checklist:

Name(s): _____

Position: _____

Name of principal at time of exploration:

_____ Date: _____

Rationale:

Why adopt looping configurations? This is perhaps the most important question you should ask yourself prior to planning and implementation. You must understand and be comfortable with the philosophy before you can effectively teach in a looping classroom. Once you determine the rationale for adoption, you can then create an evaluation plan that helps you review how it is working. Investigating looping practices is not only the first step in an effective change process, but also a crucial step toward ultimate success. The stakeholders should understand looping practices and then receive appropriate training and support.

Goals:

- Understand the vocabulary, philosophy, and instructional practices associated with looping classrooms

- Identify the benefits attributed to looping classrooms

Additional Goals:

_____

_____

_____

_____

_____

Possible Unintended Consequences of Not Doing This Step:

If this step of exploration is bypassed, stakeholders may lack philosophical grounding and skills necessary to create a looping classroom. Remember, both will and skill are the essential ingredients for success.

Why Looping?

Directions: Examine and respond to the statements in the following checklist. Check appropriate responses and use the key at the bottom of this page to help you decide which column best reflects your current situation.

I/We understand:	Yes	Some	No	Refer to Support Pages:
1) the research and vocabulary associated with looping practices and know the important differences among looping, multiage, and single-grade classrooms.				62-63 77-85
2) the advantages (benefits) and disadvantages associated with looping practices and how they pertain to my/our own setting.				77-86
3) effective management and instructional strategies used in looping classrooms.				79-85, 86
4) the role of themes and centers in numerous looping classrooms.				79-85, 86
5) the importance of using flexible grouping strategies.				62, 79-85, 86
6) how summer-bridge activities are effective components of looping classrooms.				62, 79-85, 86
Additional statements of understanding are:				
7)				
8)				

KEY:

Great! You have a working knowledge of looping practices. Proceed to Checklist 2.	**Further study is strongly recommended.** See Support Pages for suggestions.	**Further study is necessary.** See Support Pages for suggestions.

CHECKLIST 1: ✓

How Did You Learn About Looping Classrooms?

Directions: Identify the sources for your exploration step in the chart below.

Books, Research, Articles, and Studies:	School/Classroom Visitations:	"Chatrooms" Web Site/Interview:	Conferences, Seminars, In-Service Workshops:	Audiotapes, Videos, Other:

CHECKLIST 1: ✔

Assess your understanding of looping practices, then respond.

1. I/We are satisfied with our exploration of looping practices: Yes ___ No ___ Somewhat ___

2. Further investigation is needed: Yes ___ No ___

Plan to gain further experience in effective looping practices. Include who will do which activities and the date by which activities are to be completed.

_____

_____

_____

_____

_____

_____

Journal Entry/Notes _____

_____

_____

_____

_____

_____

_____

Don't forget—this space is great for notes.

CHECKLIST 2:

Is a Looping Classroom Right for You?

Person(s) responding to this checklist:

Name(s): _____

Position: _____

Name of principal at time of exploration:

_____ Date: _____

Rationale:

Is a looping classroom right for you? Now that you are familiar with the rationale, philosophy, and practices associated with looping classrooms, it is strongly recommended that you arrange opportunities to observe and try some of them first-hand. This step not only helps you make the decision about whether to create looping classrooms, but it can also help you determine staff development and/or training needs that are critical for success.

Goal(s):

- Gain first-hand experience in looping practices to determine whether or not teaching in a looping classroom is right for you

- Determine staff development and/or training needs to create the looping classrooms

Additional Goal(s):

_____

_____

_____

_____

_____

Possible Unintended Consequences of Not Doing This Step:

Teaching in a looping configuration requires skills and strategies that effectively address a group of learners that stay together for two or more years. Many teachers would agree they lack the time to effectively teach a single-grade curriculum. Without the knowledge and experience of working with different levels of curricula, as well as using specific instructional strategies that work in multiyear settings, teachers can feel overwhelmed and inadequate. This leads to potential teacher burnout and an unsuccessful looping classroom experience, which can lead to a negative community reaction.

CHECKLIST 2:  Is a Looping Classroom Right for You?

Directions: Examine and respond to the statements in the following checklist.

I/We have:	Yes	Sometimes	No	Refer to Support Pages:
1) traded places with colleagues to experience working with other ages and grade levels to observe curriculum being taught and the social/emotional development of students.				N/A
2) created temporary team-teaching opportunities with teachers at other grade levels to experience working with students and curriculum at other grade levels.				63
3) assessed my classroom management strategies and discipline procedures for their effectiveness in a multiyear looping setting.				86
4) tried using integrated, thematic instruction for one or more units of study and have set up one or more learning centers in my classroom.				62, 86
5) tried using flexible grouping strategies with my students.				62, 86
6) investigated or tried summer learning activities that bridge two grade levels together.				62, 86
Additional investigation experiences could be:				
7)				
8)				

KEY:

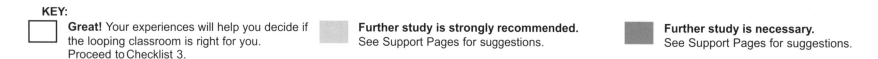

Great! Your experiences will help you decide if the looping classroom is right for you. Proceed to Checklist 3.

Further study is strongly recommended. See Support Pages for suggestions.

Further study is necessary. See Support Pages for suggestions.

How Have You Actively Explored Looping Practices?

Directions: This chart corresponds with the checklist on the previous page. Briefly record your experiences or comments in the spaces below.

Which Practices Were Tried?	With Whom?	When?	What Was Learned?

EXPLORING

CHECKLIST 2: ✔

Assess your experiences and observations, then respond.

1. I/We are satisfied with our understanding of looping practices: Yes ___ No ___
Somewhat ___

2. Further experience is needed: Yes ___ No ___

Plan to gain further experience in looping practices. Be sure to include who will do which activities and the date by which they are to be completed.

_____

_____

_____

_____

_____

Journal Entry/Notes _____

_____

_____

_____

_____

_____

_____

_____

CHECKLIST 3: ✔

Exploring Different Looping Configurations

Person(s) responding to this checklist:

Name(s): _____

Position: _____

Name of principal at time of exploration:

_____ Date: _____

Rationale:

A number of looping configurations are currently being used in schools throughout the world. One is not better than another; one simply might work better in some schools than in others. You might already know what type of looping configuration you plan to implement. If not, this checklist will help you examine both the pros and cons of each looping design. This analysis will help you make an informed decision that is right for your school.

Goal(s):

- Explore or examine the different types of possible looping configurations
- Identify the pros and cons for different looping configurations as they relate to your school to help you decide what is best for you

Additional Goal(s):

_____

_____

_____

_____

Possible Unintended Consequences of Not Doing This Step:

Not all educators are aware of the pros and cons of different kinds of looping configurations as they relate to their own schools. Since the positives and the negatives can vary from school to school, depending on each school's own set of circumstances, it is helpful to work through this analysis to be sure to implement the best possible looping configuration for your school.

Directions: Examine the different types of looping configurations listed in the following checklist. Use the chart on the next page to list the pros and cons of each type of looping configuration. Use your findings to help you make decisions about the looping design that will work best for you.

I/We have explored the pros and cons of the following looping configurations:	Yes	No	Refer to Support Pages:
1) Two-year looping			77, 81, 86
2) Three-year looping			77, 81, 86
3) Interbuilding looping			77, 81, 86
4) Half-day kindergarten/first-grade loop			77, 81, 86
5) Multiage classroom(s)			77, 78, 81, 86
6) School-within-a-school			77, 81, 86
7) Team-teaching—in any of the above configurations			77, 84, 86
Additional looping configurations to consider:			
8)			
9)			
10)			

KEY:

☐ **Great!** You have a solid understanding of looping configurations.

▨ **Check Support Pages** for definitions and suggested readings.

CHECKLIST 3:

Directions: This chart corresponds to the looping configurations listed on the previous page. As you learn about each type of configuration, list its pros and cons in the spaces provided. When finished, weigh the pros and cons to help you in your decision-making process about what is best for you.

Pros	Cons	Conclusions/Comments

CHECKLIST 3:

Assess your exploration of looping configurations, then respond.

1. I/we have weighed the pros and cons of different looping configurations to help in our decision-making process: Yes ＿＿ No ＿＿

2. Further exploration is needed: Yes ＿＿ No ＿＿

Plan to explore different types of looping configurations. Decide what configuration will work best in your school.

_____

_____

_____

_____

_____

_____

Journal Entry/Notes _____

_____

_____

_____

_____

_____

_____

"It was a little scary for me at first because I had never looped before. It might be scary for you, too. If you do it, you should remember to stay calm, be happy, and don't be scared. Looping is cool!"

— Mercedes, 8 years old
New York

PART TWO: IMPLEMENTING LOOPING CONFIGURATIONS

Designing Your Own Looping Classroom(s):

Checklist ✓ **4.** Who Needs to Know? Who Has the Expertise?

Checklist ✓ **5.** What Are Your Goals?

Checklist ✓ **6.** What Are the Essential Components of the Looping Classroom?

Preparing to Start Your Looping Classroom(s):

Checklist ✓ **7.** Which Management and Teaching Strategies Will You Incorporate?

Checklist ✓ **8.** What Are the Common Obstacles and Pitfalls to Overcome?

Beginning Your Looping Classroom(s):

Checklist ✓ **9.** How Do You Get Off to a Good Start?

IMPLEMENTING

Implementing looping practices requires careful planning. There is no one correct way or program to implement a looping configuration. Each school needs to examine its own school culture, support system, and physical space, as well as consider its school's teaching, parent, and student populations to decide what will work best for everyone.

In Part Two, the steps that lead to successful implementation of looping practices are arranged in checklist form. This implementation section guides you through the critical steps that looping educators consider or take when planning their own instructional design. If you are preparing to start looping classrooms, this step is essential. If you are already implementing looping practices, it is recommended that you review and respond to these checklist activities as part of your evaluation process.

Directions for Part Two:

1. Fill in the names and positions of persons completing each checklist.

2. Read the rationale, goal statements, and potential consequences behind each checklist. Add any additional goals of your own. Goals should be realistic and attainable.

3. Complete the checklists and chart activities to assess your current situation.

4. Create a plan to do more extensive planning for the implementation stage of the looping classroom. Refer to the Support Pages (pp. 60-86) for resources that will provide information on related looping topics.

Refer to "How to Use This Book" (p. xvi) for a completed sample checklist.

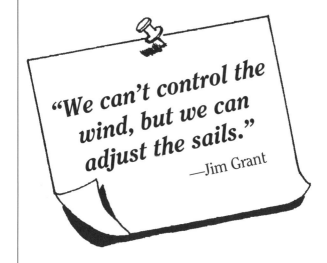

"We can't control the wind, but we can adjust the sails."

—Jim Grant

Who Needs to Know?
Who Has the Expertise?

Person(s) responding to this checklist:

Name(s): _____

Position: _____

Name of principal at time of implementation:

_____ Date: _____

Rationale:

This checklist will help you consider who has the expertise and/or authority to make decisions in regard to the implementation of looping. It will also help you identify and plan a notification and/or education process for those who need to know about it. Many people are affected directly or indirectly by the decision to implement looping, and the program's initial success can depend on when and how stakeholders are informed.

Goal(s):

- Determine who has the expertise and/or authority to make decisions about looping practices

- Determine who will be affected by your decision to implement looping classrooms

Additional Goal(s):

_____

_____

_____

_____

Possible Unintended Consequences of Not Doing This Step:

If you have not considered who has the expertise and authority to make decisions about looping, you might find that you lack the necessary support to proceed. When you do not consider who needs to be informed about your plans, you might discover that misunderstanding has become a major obstacle to your progress. Failing to plan for this step can translate into planning to fail.

IMPLEMENTING

Who Needs to Know? Who Has the Expertise?

Directions: Consider who needs to be educated, informed, and/or notified about looping. Use the charts on the following page to assess your planning for educating and notifying others about looping.

A: I/We have determined:
1)   who is responsible for making the decision(s) about looping.
2)   who has the expertise and knowledge to make good decisions about looping.
3)   who is responsible for the implementation of looping.
4)   who in the building and/or school system will be affected by this decision.

B: I/We have determined how the following groups will be educated, informed, and/or notified, if they are not already involved in this process:
5)   staff within the school (i.e., principal, colleagues, support staff, secretary, cafeteria personnel, volunteers, custodians, bus drivers, etc.)
6)   central office staff
7)   school board
8)   parents
9)   students
10)   community
Other individuals or groups who should be educated, informed, and/or notified about looping:
11)
12)

Directions: Record your responses to the checklist statements from the previous page on the charts below.

A: Names of persons responsible for or affected by statements 1–4:

B: Names of persons in 5–12	Informed	Date(s)	Not yet informed	Action to be taken	Date(s)

IMPLEMENTING

CHECKLIST 4: ✓

Assess the status of who needs to know, then respond.

1. I/We have assessed who needs to be educated, informed, and/or notified about my/our looping classroom(s): Yes ____ No ____ Somewhat ____

2. Further planning is needed: Yes ____ No ____

Plan to provide information for those who need to know about looping. Include who will do which activities and the date by which activities are to be completed.

_____

_____

_____

_____

_____

_____

Journal Entry/Notes _____

_____

_____

_____

_____

_____

CHECKLIST 5: ✓

What Are Your Goals?

Person(s) responding to this checklist:

Name(s): _____

Position: _____

Name of principal at time of implementation:

_____ Date: _____

Rationale:

Why are you implementing looping classrooms? You must consider and state your goals prior to implementation and evaluation.

Goal(s):

- Review the benefits of the looping
- Write goal statements for the looping classrooms

Additional Goal(s):

_____

_____

_____

_____

_____

Possible Unintended Consequences of Not Doing This Step:

If you do not establish why you are implementing looping, how will you know if it is working effectively? If you do not predetermine goals, how will you know what to assess and evaluate? Consequences of not writing goals might include termination of looping practices (because no one knows if it is working), or unsuccessful, ineffective looping classrooms (because an ongoing evaluation process for improvement is lacking).

CHECKLIST 5:   What Are Your Goals?

Directions: Review the list of benefits below commonly associated with looping classrooms. These benefits are more likely to occur when you establish them first as goals; you can then plan how to best achieve and measure them and provide ongoing improvement opportunities. After reviewing the goals/benefits, decide which ones you will include in your plan; then add your own. Use the chart on the next page to record your baseline data.

I/We hope to achieve a/an:
1) reduction in grade-level retentions.
2) reduction in special-education and remediation referrals.
3) reduction in discipline problems.
4) increase in students' average daily attendance.
5) improvement in individual academic performance.
6) increase in the percentage of parental involvement.
7) increase in the amount of instructional time, gained through eliminating the start-of-school redundancy.
8) improvement in students' independent learning and study skills.
9) more integrated, continuous-progress curriculum, including summer learning.
Additional goal statements are:
10)
11)
12)

Directions: Check the **Not at This Time** or the **Yes** column to indicate which goals you hope to achieve through implementing the looping classroom(s). Research the current baseline data for each goal. (Check with the administrative office for numerical baseline data or write descriptions of the current situation for non-numerical baseline information.)

Not at This Time	Yes	Baseline Data/Description	Source (numerical, anecdotal/observational)

IMPLEMENTING

CHECKLIST 5:

Assess your goals and the available baseline data, then respond.

1. I/We have established current goals for our looping classroom(s): Yes ____ No ____

2. Further goal setting and gathering of baseline data are needed: Yes ____ No ____

Plan for establishing goals and gathering baseline data/information. Include who will do which activities and the date by which activities are to be completed.

_____

_____

_____

_____

_____

Journal Entry/Notes _____

_____

_____

_____

_____

_____

CHECKLIST 6: ✔

What Are the Essential Components of the Looping Classroom?

Person(s) responding to this checklist:
Name(s): _____
Position: _____
Name of principal at time of implementation:
_____ Date: _____

Rationale:

Specific components need to be considered when creating looping classrooms. These are the nuts and bolts that need to be in place and adjusted prior to starting.

Goal(s):

- Identify and plan for critical components in your classroom(s)
- Determine a student selection process
- Determine parental involvement in the selection process
- Plan how curriculum will be addressed
- Consider how core materials will be shared
- Determine whether or not to change classrooms during the looping process

Additional Goal(s):

_____

_____

_____

_____

_____

Possible Unintended Consequences of Not Doing This Step:

With insufficient preparation, implementing looping classrooms might be an unsuccessful experience. Sometimes, we overlook the more obvious—yet the most essential—components in the implementation process. The items in Checklist 6 are critical starting points in your planning.

IMPLEMENTING

Directions: Examine the statements listed below, then add your own essential components. Record your responses to this checklist on the corresponding chart.

I/We have planned:
1) which grades will loop.
2) which teachers and support-staff members will teach in the looping classrooms.
3) how students will be selected for the looping classrooms.
4) how parents will be involved in the looping classroom process.
5) how core materials/resources will be shared for effective implementation.
6) whether or not teachers will change classrooms in the loop.
7) how to effectively plan curriculum for two years, including summer learning.
Additional components are:
8)
9)
10)

KEY:

[ ] **Great!** You have considered the essential looping components. Continue with your implementation. Before proceeding to Checklist 7, complete the chart on the next page.

Further planning for essential looping components is necessary.
See Support Pages for suggestions.

CHECKLIST 6:

Directions: This checklist corresponds to the essential looping components on the previous page. Mark either the **Yes** or the **Not at This Time** column, according to which response best reflects your own level of preparedness for implementation. Record the specifics for the components on the spaces provided in the chart.

Yes	Describe Specific Components:	Not at This Time	Refer to Support Pages:
			70-72, 86
			70-72, 86
			66, 67, 70-72, 86
			66, 67, 68, 69, 73-75, 82-84
			70-72, 86
			70-72, 86
			70-72, 86

IMPLEMENTING

CHECKLIST 6:

Assess the status of your planning for the components of your looping classroom(s), then respond.

1. I/We have assessed and planned for the components necessary for effective implementation of the looping classroom(s): Yes ____ No ____ Somewhat ____

2. Further planning is needed: Yes ____ No ____

Plan for the essential components for the looping classroom. Include who will do which activities and the date by which activities are to be completed.

_____

_____

_____

_____

_____

Journal Entry/Notes _____

_____

_____

_____

_____

_____

CHECKLIST 7:

Which Management and Teaching Strategies Will You Incorporate?

Person(s) responding to this checklist:

Name(s): _____

Position: _____

Name of principal at time of implementation:

_____ Date: _____

Rationale:

Today's classrooms require instructional and management strategies that support a diverse range of learners. When teachers loop for two or more years, it is more important than ever to be trained in effective teaching practices where cooperation, interdependence, and independence are nurtured and reinforced. Teaching in such a classroom requires specific staff development training in the strategies listed in Checklist 7. It cannot be assumed that a teacher has the time and skills to learn everything "on the job."

Goal(s):

- Assess teacher-training needs for effective classroom management techniques
- Assess teacher-training needs for effective classroom instructional strategies

Additional Goal(s):

_____

_____

_____

_____

_____

Possible Unintended Consequences of Not Doing This Step:

Without appropriate staff development or training, teachers might find themselves lacking in the skills necessary to teach in a looping classroom. This leads to teacher and student frustration, and an unsuccessful looping experience.

IMPLEMENTING

Directions: Examine the statements below, then record your responses on the corresponding chart on the next page.

I/We have planned for these management and teaching strategies:

1) a positive, cooperative discipline approach

2) learning centers

3) classroom rules and routines

4) integrated and thematic instruction

5) grouping variations: large group instruction   flexible grouping
   cooperative learning
   individual work

6) multiple-intelligence theory

7) technology use

8) team teaching

9) authentic assessment/evaluation

10) hands-on math and science

11) process writing

12) literature-based reading

13) summer learning strategies/activities

Additional strategies and activities are:

14)

15)

KEY:

☐ **Great!** Your teaching and management strategies will work well in a looping classroom.

▨ **Further staff development and training will be helpful for success.**

▧ **Further staff development and training will be necessary for successful implementation.**

CHECKLIST 7:

Directions: This checklist corresponds to the management and instructional statements on the previous page. Mark the columns that best reflect your current situation, then assess your level of preparedness for implementation.

Yes	In Process	Not at This Time	Refer to Support Pages:	Comments:
			79-86	
			79-86	
			79-86	
			79-86	
			62, 79-86	
			79-86	
			82-83, 84	
			62, 78	
			62, 78	
			78, 79, 80	
			78, 79, 80	
			78, 79, 80	
			78	

IMPLEMENTING

CHECKLIST 7: ✓

Assess the status of your training and preparedness for the management and teaching strategies you will incorporate, then respond.

1. I/We have assessed and prepared for the management and teaching strategies to be incorporated in my/our looping classroom(s): Yes ____ No ____ Somewhat ____

2. Further staff development and training are needed: Yes ____ No ____

Plan for future staff development and training. Include who will do which activities and the date by which activities are to be completed.

_____

_____

_____

_____

_____

Journal Entry/Notes _____

_____

_____

_____

_____

_____

_____

_____

CHECKLIST 8: ✓

What Are the Common Obstacles and Pitfalls to Overcome?

Person(s) responding to this checklist:

Name(s): _____

Position: _____

Name of principal at time of implementation:

_____ Date: _____

Rationale:

There are certain obstacles and pitfalls that often impede the implementation of looping classrooms. An important task is to find ways to work around or eliminate these obstacles as part of your implementation process. You must understand, however, that eliminating or avoiding all pitfalls might be unrealistic and unattainable.

Goal(s):

- Identify potential obstacles and pitfalls that might impede your implementation of looping classrooms

- Plan ways to avoid, minimize, or eliminate these obstacles and pitfalls

Additional Goal(s):

_____

_____

_____

_____

Possible Unintended Consequences of Not Doing This Step:

Reports of unsuccessful looping experiences frequently include many of the obstacles and pitfalls cited in Checklist 8. It is important to be proactive and to plan for as many known or foreseeable obstacles as possible. It is not how quickly you implement looping, but rather how effectively. If you do not address the obstacles, you may find it extremely difficult to implement looping classrooms, and you could possibly lose the confidence of the stakeholders whose support is necessary for effective implementation.

CHECKLIST 8:

What Are the Common Obstacles and Pitfalls to Overcome?

Directions: Examine the obstacles and pitfalls to looping classrooms listed below, then record your responses on the corresponding chart on the next page.

I/We have considered, planned, and prepared for these potential obstacles and pitfalls:
1) insufficient planning for implementation and lack of timeline
2) implementing too quickly—lack of understanding of the change process
3) mandating looping classrooms
4) starting for the wrong reasons (e.g., financial, "cutting edge" concept, etc.)
5) staff dissension
6) class composition (student population) imbalance (e.g., too many special-education students placed in room)
7) frequent adoption of new curriculum programs and materials
8) insufficient support from administrators, colleagues, parents, etc.
9) insufficient training and ongoing staff development to support looping practices
10) incompatible evaluation and assessment strategies
11) poor communication with colleagues, parents, and community members
Additional obstacles or pitfalls are:
12)
13)
14)

KEY:

Great! Continue with your implementation, but always be proactive when considering obstacles and pitfalls.

Further planning for obstacles and pitfalls is recommended for success. See Support Pages for suggestions.

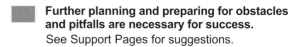

Further planning and preparing for obstacles and pitfalls are necessary for success. See Support Pages for suggestions.

CHECKLIST 8:

Directions: Mark the columns that best reflect your own situation, then assess your level of preparedness for implementation. Record your action plan to avoid or minimize obstacles and pitfalls you face.

Yes	In Process	Not Prepared at This Time	Refer to Support Pages:	Action Planned to Avoid or Minimize Obstacles and Pitfalls
			86	
			86	
			86	
			86	
			86	
			86	
			86	
			86	
			86	
			86	
			86	

CHECKLIST 8: ✔

Assess the common obstacles and pitfalls as they relate to your situation, then respond.

1. I/We have assessed and planned for the obstacles and pitfalls we face at this time:
   Yes ___ No ___ Somewhat ___

2. Further planning for these obstacles and pitfalls is needed: Yes ___ No ___

Plan to avoid or minimize obstacles and pitfalls to the looping classroom. Include who will do which activities and the date by which activities are to be completed.

_____

_____

_____

_____

Journal Entry/Notes _____

_____

_____

_____

_____

_____

CHECKLIST 9: ✔

How Do You Get Off to a Good Start?

Person(s) responding to this checklist:

Name(s): _____

Position: _____

Name of principal at time of implementation:

_____ Date: _____

Rationale:

First things first! Beginnings can produce excitement and anxiety. The better prepared you are, the less you will worry. It is critical to carefully plan for the first day, the first week, and the first staff and parent meetings.

Goal(s):

- Plan for classroom "firsts"

- Plan for building/school-system "firsts"

Additional Goal(s):

_____

_____

_____

_____

_____

Possible Unintended Consequences of Not Doing This Step:

Without this planning, you can get caught up in the hectic "business as usual," and perhaps get off to a difficult start. First impressions are important when beginning looping. Getting off to a good start by planning your first day and week in the classroom, your first meeting with parents, and your first faculty meeting can have lasting positive effects.

How Do You Get Off to a Good Start? What Are the Firsts?

Directions: Examine the "firsts" below, then record your responses at right and on the corresponding chart on the next page.

I/We have planned and prepared for my/our:	Yes	In Process	Not Prepared at This Time
1) first instructional day			
2) first instructional week			
3) first parent conference/meeting			
4) first parent newsletter			
5) first open house			
6) first faculty meeting			
Additional "firsts" are:			
7)			
8)			
9)			

KEY:

| | Great! You are prepared for a good start. |

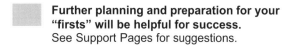 **Further planning and preparation for your "firsts" will be helpful for success.** See Support Pages for suggestions.

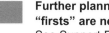 **Further planning and preparation for your "firsts" are necessary for success.** See Support Pages for suggestions.

CHECKLIST 9: ✔

Directions: After marking the columns on the previous page that best reflect your own situation, record a brief plan and timeline for implementing your "firsts."

Brief Plan and Timeline for "Firsts":

IMPLEMENTING

CHECKLIST 9: ✔

Assess the status of your planning and preparation for the "firsts" in your looping classroom, then respond.

1. I/We have assessed, planned, and prepared for the critical "firsts" for the looping classroom(s): Yes ___ No ___ Somewhat ___

2. Further planning and preparation are needed: Yes ___ No ___

Plan for "firsts" in your looping classroom(s). Include who will do which activities and the date by which activities are to be completed.

_____

_____

_____

_____

Journal Entry/Notes _____

_____

_____

_____

_____

_____

PART THREE: EVALUATING LOOPING CONFIGURATIONS

EVALUATING

"Experience is not what happens to a man.
It is what a man does with what happens to him."

—Aldous Huxley

Evaluating looping classrooms allows you to determine what has or has not worked. Which components are working well? Which need revision or refocus? These are important questions to ask during this process. To many, however, "evaluation" implies something that needs to be completed, something to get out of the way. Yet evaluation is what helps us improve; it keeps us from stagnating.

This section will help you establish an evaluation process for your looping instructional design. It will clarify which elements need to be evaluated and how the results should be used, shared, and reported.

The evaluation process we recommend is as follows:
1. Review your goals
2. Select goals you want to evaluate
3. Select your sources of data
4. Develop your evaluation plan
5. Collect data
6. Analyze data
7. Consider your progress toward goals and/or revisions

Directions for Part Three:

1. Fill in the names and positions of persons completing each checklist.
2. Read the rationale, goal statements, and consequences. Add any additional goals of your own. Goals should be realistic and attainable.
3. Complete the checklists and chart activities to assess and plan your evaluation process.
4. Create a plan to fill in gaps or complete necessary steps to achieve a successful evaluation process.

Refer to "How to Use This Book" (p. xvi) for a completed sample checklist.

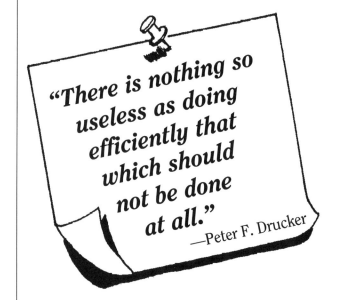

"There is nothing so useless as doing efficiently that which should not be done at all."
—Peter F. Drucker

CHECKLIST 10: ✔

What Are S.M.A.R.T. Goals?
Are Your Goals Smart?

Person(s) responding to this checklist:

Name(s): _____

Position: _____

Name of principal at time of evaluation:

_____ Date: _____

Rationale:

Developing goals that are **S**pecific, **M**easurable, **A**ttainable, **R**elevant and **R**ealistic, and **T**ime specific is an important step in the evaluation process. Assessment and evaluation drive what you deem important in your looping classroom(s). For this reason, goals themselves need to be assessed for their effectiveness.

Goal(s):

- Understand the meaning of S.M.A.R.T. goals
- Assess looping goals to see if they fit the S.M.A.R.T. criteria

Additional Goal(s):

_____

_____

_____

_____

Possible Unintended Consequences of Not Doing This Step:

Unrealistic goals often lead to failure. How often have you heard of goals that are unattainable or not relevant? When you assess your goals with the S.M.A.R.T. criteria, your implementation and evaluation process is based on realistic expectations and is more likely to be successful.

EVALUATING

CHECKLIST 10:

What Are S.M.A.R.T. Goals? Are Your Goals Smart?

Directions: Refer to Checklist 5 to review your goals and to decide which goals you will assess and evaluate. Next, write the chosen goals below. Read the criteria for S.M.A.R.T. goals identified on the chart on the next page. Use the chart/checklist on the following page to assess each goal statement using the S.M.A.R.T. criteria.

Goals to assess and evaluate:
1)
2)
3)
4)
5)
6)

CHECKLIST 10: ✓   What Are S.M.A.R.T. Goals? Are Your Goals Smart?

Directions: Use the checklist below to assess each goal with the S.M.A.R.T. criteria. Begin with Goal 1 in the first column, then continue using the criteria to assess all your goals. Check each box in the column only if it is true. Leave the box blank if the goal does not meet the criteria.

	Goal 1	Goal 2	Goal 3	Goal 4	Goal 5	Goal 6
Each goal is **Specific** ("This is what we need to do.")						
Each goal is **Measurable** ("This is how we will know we have done it.")						
Each goal is **Attainable** ("This is why I'm confident we can do it.")						
Each goal is **Relevant** and **Realistic** ("This is why it must and can/should be done.")						
Each goal is **Time** specific ("This is when we need to do it.")						

EVALUATING

CHECKLIST 10:

Are your goals smart? Assess your results, then respond.

1. I/We are satisfied that the goal statements meet the S.M.A.R.T. criteria: Yes ___ No ___
Somewhat ___

2. Further consideration or revision of goals is necessary: Yes ___ No ___

Revised goals/plan to ensure they are S.M.A.R.T. Include who will do which activities and the date by which activities are to be completed.

_____

_____

_____

_____

_____

Journal Entry/Notes _____

_____

_____

_____

_____

_____

_____

CHECKLIST 11:

What Are the Possible Sources of Information?

Rationale:

When collecting data for your evaluation process, there are many valuable sources to consider, including surveys, questionnaires, and attendance records. It is important to match the source of data with the type of information you need to gather. This step will help you identify your sources of information based on the goals you have established.

Goal(s):

- Identify potential sources of data or information

- Choose the sources that will assist you in evaluating each looping goal

- Identify persons responsible for creating, distributing, and collecting sources of information

Additional Goal(s):

_____

_____

_____

_____

_____

Possible Unintended Consequences of Not Doing This Step:

Smart evaluation requires smart planning. If you do not predetermine your sources of information, you might find yourself unable to measure your progress.

EVALUATING

CHECKLIST 11: ✔ What Are the Possible Sources of Information?

Directions: Examine the possible sources of information for your evaluation process. Decide which sources best suit each of the looping goals that you choose from the checklists. Check each box that identifies an information source for each goal. On the next page, use the chart to determine the current status of these sources of information.

I/We will use the following information sources:	Goal 1	Goal 2	Goal 3	Goal 4	Goal 5	Goal 6
1) interviews						
2) surveys						
3) questionnaires						
4) journals						
5) checklists						
6) student records						
7) attendance records						
8) retention records						
9) special-education referrals						
10) discipline referrals						
11) observations						
12) videotapes						
Additional sources of information are:						
13)						
14)						
15)						

CHECKLIST 11: ✓

Directions: This chart corresponds with the sources of information on the checklist on the previous page. Check the box that best reflects the current status of your information sources.

Sources Are in Place	Person(s) Responsible	Sources Not Yet in Place	Person(s) Responsible to Have in Place	Projected Date

CHECKLIST 11:

Assess the status of your data sources, then respond.

1. I/We are satisfied with the status of our data sources: Yes ___ No ___ Somewhat ___

2. Further planning is needed for the sources of data: Yes ___ No ___

Plan to identify the sources of information needed for the evaluation process. Include who will do which activities and the date by which activities are to be completed.

_____

_____

_____

_____

_____

Journal Entry/Notes _____

_____

_____

_____

_____

_____

CHECKLIST 12: ✓

How Will Results of the Evaluation Process Be Used?

Person(s) responding to this checklist:

Name(s): _____

Position: _____

Name of principal at time of evaluation:

_____ Date: _____

Rationale:

Why complete the entire evaluation process if you have no plans to use or share the information? A plan for continual improvement and necessary revisions is a key reason to implement an evaluation process. The information gained is the basis for changing or improving the existing program. By reading and completing this step you bring your looping process full circle. It provides you with your own data for measuring and assessing the effectiveness of your looping configurations.

Goal(s):

- Identify how the evaluation process results will be used
- Determine how the evaluation results will be shared

Additional Goal(s):

_____

_____

_____

_____

Possible Unintended Consequences of Not Doing This Step:

The evaluation process is not an end in itself, but rather the critical pivot point at which you make decisions on necessary revisions or improvements for your looping classroom(s). You must also decide with whom you will share your findings. Failing to complete this step is analogous to assessing a student's academic needs in the classroom and then filing away the results without doing anything to improve and share the student's progress.

EVALUATING

How Will Results of the Evaluation Process Be Used?

Directions: Place a check in the box that corresponds with your current status for each statement below. Use the chart on the next page to record how and with whom your results will be shared.

I/We have determined:	Yes	Not Yet	Comments
1) how frequently we will assess progress toward each goal.			
2) how we will refine or adjust our looping classroom(s) based on our ongoing assessment and evaluation.			
3) with whom we will share the results of our ongoing evaluation process.			
4) the person(s) responsible for sharing our findings.			
5) how our evaluation information will be shared (e.g., newspaper, newsletter, parent meeting, teacher meeting, etc.).			
Additional goals for using and sharing evaluation results are:			
6)			
7)			

KEY:

☐ **Great!** You have planned how the results of your evaluation process will be used and shared.

▨ **Answers to these statements are necessary for an effective evaluation process.**

CHECKLIST 12: ✔

Directions: This chart is a tool to be used with the checklist on the previous page. Write your plans for how your ongoing evaluation will be used and with whom you will share it.

Looping Goals	Purpose of Evaluation: How Will the Results Be Used?	How Will the Results Be Shared?

EVALUATING

CHECKLIST 12: ✓

Assess how you will use and share the results of your findings, then respond.

1. I/We are satisfied with how we plan to use our findings: Yes ___ No ___ Somewhat ___

2. Further planning for this part of the evaluation is needed: Yes ___ No ___

Plan to use and share your evaluation results. Include who will do which activities and the date by which activities are to be completed.

_____

_____

_____

_____

_____

Journal Entry/Notes _____

_____

_____

_____

_____

_____

_____

CHECKLIST 13: ✓

Putting It All Together: Assessing the Steps Toward a Successful Evaluation Process

Person(s) responding to this checklist:

Name(s): _____

Position: _____

Name of principal at time of evaluation:

_____ Date: _____

Rationale:

In checklists 10, 11, and 12, you assessed your goals with S.M.A.R.T. criteria, chose the sources of information to evaluate your goals, and determined how you will use and share your findings. This step helps you put it all together on a chart to create a holistic overview of your evaluation process. This checklist is a final proofreading of the steps you have taken toward implementing a successful looping classroom.

Goal(s):

- Consider the steps for a successful evaluation plan

- Develop an effective evaluation plan for the looping classroom

Additional Goal(s):

_____

_____

_____

_____

_____

Possible Unintended Consequences of Not Doing This Step:

What happens when you don't evaluate? You have been working on this question throughout this book, but now what is needed is a project timeline. The activities in this checklist provide the "big picture" that will help you put everything together in your evaluation process. Without a holistic view of your evaluation process, it is difficult to see the interrelatedness and timeliness of all the different components.

EVALUATING

CHECKLIST 13:

Putting It All Together: Assessing the Steps Toward a Successful Evaluation Process

Directions: Examine the steps for a successful evaluation process listed in the checklist below. These steps were previously described in the introduction to Part Three. It is time to revisit them and assess your current status. Write a check in each box that best describes your current status with each statement. Use the chart on the next page to create a holistic view of your complete plan and timeline.

I/We have:	Yes	In Process	Not Yet	Expected Date for Completion
1) reviewed our goals for the looping classroom.				
2) selected the goals we want to evaluate.				
3) selected our sources of data.				
4) developed an evaluation plan.				
5) collected data.				
6) analyzed the data.				
7) considered our progress toward goals and/or revisions.				

KEY:

☐ **Great!** If you have checked this column, you are in an excellent position to make good decisions about your looping classroom(s).

▨ **Review the checklists in Part Three to be sure you are on track.**

▨ **Complete the checklists in Part Three to help you achieve these steps.** If you have addressed these steps, obtain a progress report from the person responsible for completing the activity.

What Are the Steps for a Successful Evaluation Process?

Directions: This chart will provide a holistic overview of the evaluation steps listed in the checklist on the previous page. You can 1) use it "as is" to fill in your responses, 2) enlarge it to a greater, desirable size, or 3) create a spreadsheet to chart your complete plan.

	Goal	Data Source	Person Responsible	Steps to Completion	Timeline	Who Needs to Know?
EXAMPLE	90% of parents will agree that the second year was less stressful for their child.	Parent Survey	School Secretary	1. Locate and duplicate survey. 2. Send to parents with SASE. 3. Collate results. 4. Share with teachers.	Send: 4/30 Return: 5/15	Teachers/Parents School Board

EVALUATING

CHECKLIST 13: ✔

Assess your progress to evaluate each goal. Where are the gaps, if any? What needs to be done? Consider these points, then respond.

1. I/We are satisfied with the plan for our evaluation process: Yes ___ No ___ Somewhat ___

2. Further development of the plan is needed: Yes ___ No ___

Plan to address gaps or questions related to your evaluation plan. Include who will do which activities and the date by which activities are to be completed.

_____

_____

_____

_____

_____

Journal Entry/Notes _____

_____

_____

_____

_____

_____

_____

PART FOUR: SUPPORT PAGES

✓ Contents and Purpose

✓ Looping Glossary

✓ Sample Pages for Parents

✓ Parent/Teacher Questionnaires and Reproducibles

✓ References and Recommended Resources

✓ Biblio-Index

SUPPORT PAGES

Welcome to the Support Pages! As you worked through the checklists and charts, you might have checked items that referred you to this section. These pages direct you to specific resources where you can obtain more information or read further about a specific topic or component concerning the looping classroom. Some direct you to sources for specific information, and others are sample reproducible forms for you to use in your looping evaluation process.

Included are reproducible sample surveys, letters, questionnaires, forms, and charts. Time is a precious resource, and these examples are provided to help you avoid starting everything from scratch. The samples are here for you to revise and use to meet your own needs.

Contents and Purpose

Glossary of Looping and Multiage Terms:
Use this to broaden your understanding of looping and multiage terms.

"If I decide to loop, should I stay in the same room for two years, or should I move to a new room for the second year?" (excerpt from *Looping Q&A*, 1997)

Sample Parent Letters (Fall and Spring):
These introductory letters to looping can be revised to accommodate your own situation.

Parent Questionnaire for Placement:
This form requests parental input to help in the student placement process. It provides an opportunity for parents to offer information about how their children learn. It does not, however, allow parents to choose a specific teacher.

Sign-Up/Opt-Out Form (English and Spanish):
This form provides a way for parents to request that their child be considered for placement in a looping classroom. It also serves as an "insurance policy" to allow the parents or school to opt out of the looping classroom if a more appropriate placement is in the best interest of a student.

Time is a precious resource, and these examples are provided to help you avoid starting everything from scratch.

Student Placement Plan and Chart:
This process will help you set up balanced classrooms for multiage, looping, and single-year configurations (excerpt from *Looping Q&A*, pp. 86-88).

Parental Involvement Assessment Tool:
This chart helps you assess the number and types of activities you use to involve parents in your school community.

Bilingual Surveys:
  • Looping Survey for Parents (English and Spanish)
  • Looping Survey for Teachers

These surveys can be revised or are ready to use as sources of information for your evaluation process.

References and Recommended Resources:
  • Web Sites
  • Videos and Study Kits
  • Sources of Data and Information

Biblio-Index

LOOPING GLOSSARY

authentic assessment: Assessment that demonstrates a child's actual learning in the classroom. An authentic assessment tool, such as a student writing portfolio, documents a student's process and progress over time.

combination grade/split grade (sometimes called multigrade): Two or more distinct grades in one classroom that are taught as separate entities. Instruction and assessment are separate for each grade. Reasons for creating this configuration are generally not pedagogical; rather, they are created out of economic necessity (due to low or uneven enrollment numbers or budget constraints). These are not considered true multiage configurations.

continuous progress: Students work at their individual learning rates. In a nongraded multiage school, there are no letter grades, retentions, or promotions. In today's typical multiage configuration, students progress toward academic goals over a two-or-more-year time period.

flexible grouping: Flexible groups are created to accommodate a diverse range of learners and interests in the classroom. These groups are designed for specific purposes and are usually temporary in nature, with a group disbanding or students leaving the group when a set goal has been reached. Students learn to work together for a variety of purposes, in a variety of settings, with a variety of learners. Examples of flexible groups include skills, interest, cooperative, and study.

interbuilding looping: When a teacher from an exit grade of one school progresses with his/her class to the next grade at the entry level of another school, the practice is called interbuilding looping. (For example, in a K–3 school and a 4–6 school in the same school system, the third- and fourth-grade teachers would form a partnership and loop between buildings.) Schools and teachers adopt this configuration to ease the transition for students between schools, instead of between grade levels within a school. Generally, each teacher in this situation has one evaluator: the principal from his/her "home" school. Interbuilding looping partners change schools every other year and generally share classroom materials to avoid frequent moving.

learning centers: Learning centers are designated places in the classroom where specific materials and activities are available to allow students opportunities to explore, practice, or extend their understanding of concepts and skills. Learning centers can be permanent, temporary, or portable in nature. They might be set up according to content areas, including math, reading, science, writing, listening, and social studies. Teachers might also arrange their classrooms into centers that include their daily routines, curriculum, and interests. Used as an instructional and management strategy, learning centers allow teachers to meet with an individual or a small group (flexible group), while other students in the classroom are engaged in preplanned, purposeful learning.

looping: Looping is a multiyear instructional design that places a single grade of students together for two or more years with the same teacher(s). The purposes of looping are building long-term relationships and gaining more effective use of instructional time. Other terms synonymous with looping are student-teacher progression, teacher rotation, and multiyear teaching. Teachers either rotate between classrooms or remain in the same classroom, involving their students in the room setup for the next grade level, while exchanging core materials with their partners.

multiage: Multiage is a multiyear instructional design that blends two or more grades together into a single classroom of learners with the same teacher(s) for two or more years. The multiage philosophy focuses on looking at children in more of a "real-world" view by creating a class with a wide range of ages where peer teaching (tutoring), long-term relationships, and continuous-progress practices are attainable goals. Multiage is cyclical teaching and is a complex form of looping.

multiyear: The multiyear classroom is where students are taught by the same teacher(s) for two or more years. Looping and multiage classrooms are both examples of multiyear configurations. This concept is not to be confused with combination-grade/split-grade configurations.

nongraded (also ungraded): Nongraded schooling is an idealistic philosophy in today's graded world of schooling. It is a design that focuses on continuous-progress learning for individual students and eliminates graded practices such as grade-level designations, comparative reporting (A, B, C, D, F grades), tracking, retention, promotion, social promotion, group standardized tests, and age-/grade-specific standards.

peer tutoring: This practice capitalizes on the belief that to teach another is the highest form of understanding. It is practiced by educators who believe everyone in the classroom both teaches and learns. The student doing the peer tutoring is not meant to be a "teacher's aide," but rather someone who can assist another child's learning while reinforcing his or her own.

school-within-a-school: When a large school reconfigures itself into smaller units within the school, a school-within-a-school is created. In this type of setting, schools that are typically separated into areas according to grade-level designation might reconfigure into teams or communities of multiple-grade groupings. For example, a traditional K–4 school, with four sections of each grade, might be assigned to five specific grade areas. If they change to a school-within-a-school, they would create four learning teams or communities, each containing K–4 classrooms. Students would remain in their learning communities from kindergarten through fourth grade. Most schools create this configuration to facilitate long-term relationships among students, parents, and teachers. Each school-within-a-school can also address diversity in teaching philosophies. One community might use a multiage instructional design, another looping, and another single-year, single-grade classrooms.

summer bridge: In a multiage or looping classroom, students learn together with the same teacher(s) for two or more years. In both of these configurations, the summer offers opportunities for students to work on a variety of activities and studies that will bridge the two school years (see *The Looping Handbook*, 1996).

team teaching: When two or more teachers plan together and share the responsibility of teaching the same group of students, they are team teaching. They might be located in the same room or teach their own class in an adjacent or nearby room, teaming for some or all of the instruction.

three-way or student-led conferences: When the student, teacher, and parent(s) all meet at the same time to discuss the student's progress and set future goals, the process is called three-way conferencing. This method is used to encourage the parent to become an active partner in the student's education. A three-way conference with the student actually leading the session is known as a student-led conference.

Q. If I decide to loop, should I stay in the same room for two years, or should I move to a new room for the second year?

A. The decision concerning this frequently asked question is best left to the teachers involved.

Some actually move their classrooms to accommodate parents who want their children to feel promoted to another classroom for the second year. Other teachers choose to stay in the same room, primarily because they have so much "stuff" that it would be a hardship to move.

Usually, teachers who remain in the same classroom are careful to change key components in the room. In fact, at the end of the first year, we suggest that looping teachers involve their students in May or June, by asking them to design what they would like their classroom to look like the second year. This typical "down" time in June can be put to good use by empowering students to prepare next year's folders, portfolios, journals, reading logs, classroom environment, etc.

When deciding how to handle classroom space assignments, it is important to remember that each school has its own individual circumstances to consider. Here are some thoughts for both options:

Reasons to Consider Remaining in the Same Classroom

- You will be using most of your own materials, and it would be a true hardship to move them.
- There is no strong reason for moving, and it would use up valuable energy and time.
- The physical space is appropriate for your teaching style.
- If only a few teachers are looping, you might prefer to stay in your own classroom if it does not greatly affect the dynamics of your class in relation to the rest of the school. For example, if you teach third grade, then loop to fourth, will it matter if students remain in your classroom, while other third graders move to another area of the building for fourth grade? In some schools this is a concern, while in others it is not.

Reasons to Consider Changing Classrooms

- If you have a kindergarten/first grade loop, it is advisable to ensure that kindergartners be in a physical space that is developmentally appropriate for their needs.
- You and your partner are comfortable sharing the bulk of the materials. The materials can remain and the teachers move, particularly when classrooms are assigned in groups according to grade level.
- If only a few teachers are looping in a school with designated grade-level wings, you might choose to move if it is important for students to be with their peers. You might also want to be with other teachers at your grade level; there are times when teachers feel left out of grade-level decisions and activities when they are in a different physical space.

Sample Letter to Parents: Looping Information Meeting — Beginning of the Year

September 25

Dear Parents,

How often have you wished your children could remain with their teacher(s) for more than one year? During the past year, we have been investigating an instructional design called "looping." This means that the same class of students is taught by the same teacher or team of teachers for two consecutive years.

There are compelling reasons to consider looping. We would like to share these with you on October 1 (Wednesday) at 7:00 p.m. in the school library. We also want to listen to any questions and concerns you might have about looping.

We are pleased that a number of teachers at our school are presently studying this concept and are interested in implementing this two-year cycle of teaching, beginning with the next school year.

We look forward to meeting with you and discussing this student-centered concept of spending two years with the same teacher. If you cannot attend, please feel free to call me for information. Thank you!

Sincerely,

Principal

May 22

Dear Parents,

I couldn't let the school year draw to a close without commenting on what I believe has been an exciting and productive year!

I am also writing to let you know that your child will progress to fourth grade with me in a "looping configuration." Looping, or student/teacher progression, is an instructional design that allows me to teach students over a two-year time period.

The benefits of having the same teacher for two years are quite extraordinary. Your child and I have developed a relationship that will only continue to grow. We have begun to establish trust and understanding, which form the foundation to a powerful learning atmosphere. Also, consider the academic growth that can take place immediately upon arrival in the fall, because students are already familiar with everyday classroom procedures. These benefits are just a few of many! This is a very exciting option.

There are pros and cons to every issue, though. One con could be that you/your child is not comfortable with my teaching style or me. If that is the case, please let the principal or me know as soon as possible so we can place your child appropriately next year.

If you have questions/concerns, please feel free to call the principal or me. Thank you! I look forward to seeing you in the fall!

Sincerely,

Teacher

Sample Parent Questionnaire*
for Student Placement

Dear Parent or Guardian:

The staff is about to begin the student placement process for next year. We devote our expertise and time toward creating classroom assignments that ensure balance for optimal teaching and learning, and we invite you to share your thoughts—impressions so valuable to us—about your child's needs. If you would like to participate in this process, please return your questionnaire no later than April 1.

Thanks so much for your help! We look forward to reading your comments.

Child's Name: _____   Date: _____

Check all the statements that are true about your child:

____1. likes frequent change   ____5. likes predictability
____2. prefers to work alone   ____6. prefers group work
____3. likes teacher direction   ____7. likes to be independent
____4. has difficulty with transitions ____8. adapts easily to change

Please write any other information (not confidential) you would like to share about your child:

_____

_____

_____

_____

_____

_____

_____

Parent's Name   Date

*Survey adapted from questionnaire in *How to Change to a Nongraded School* by Madeline Hunter. The Association for Supervision and Curriculum Development ©1992

SIGN-UP AND "OPT-OUT" FORM

My child's name: _____

My child's grade next fall:_____

    I would like my child to be <u>considered</u> for placement in a looping class-room, beginning with the _____ school year.
                               (year)

OPT-OUT CLAUSE:
    I understand that if my child is selected to be in a looping classroom, he/she will have the same teacher(s) for two school years.
    I also understand that at the end of the first school year, either the school or I can choose a more appropriate placement for my child without consequence.

_____
Parent/Guardian Signature   Date

A REPRODUCIBLE FORM

FORMULARIO DE FIRMAR O REHUSIR

Nombre de mi hijo/a:_____

Grado de mi hijo/a el próximo otoño:

_____

Quisiera que se <u>considere</u> colocar a mi hijo/a en una clase enlazada (o sea, una en que su hijo/a se quedaría con el/la mismo/a maestro/a y compañeros de clase por 2 años), empezando con el año escolar _____ .

CLÁUSULA DE REHUSIR:
   Comprendo que si mi hijo/a se seleccione para la clase enlazada, él/ella tendrá el/la mismo/a maestro/a por dos o más años escolares.
   También comprendo que al fin del año escolar, o la escuela o yo pueda escoger una clase más apropiada para mi hijo/a sin consecuencia.

Firma del Padre o Tutor _____   Fecha _____

Q.

What is a good student selection process for a looping classroom?

A. First, you need to ask yourself some questions. Who is presently involved in making student selection decisions? Do you have guidelines in place? Will looping require changing those guidelines?

If you don't have guidelines, or if they need to be revised or updated, a team of teachers and administrators should be formed to work on them.

Here are some considerations in drawing up student placement guidelines:

- Make sure you balance your classroom in terms of student population (see pp. 71-72).
- If teachers spend time in the spring placing children in balanced classes, make sure that those placements are not changed over the summer, so teachers don't return to completely different groups.
- Address the placement of new and incoming students to maintain balanced classrooms.
- Establish a "getting to know you" period of time in the fall of the first year. This is especially helpful for new, incoming second-year students and allows for proactive changes.
- Have an "opting-out" policy in place at the end of the first year to allow parents the choice of removing their child from the looping classroom if they're unsatisfied with the arrangement.

Once they're completed, it is important that your guidelines appear in writing and are known and understood by teachers and parents.

Excerpted from *Looping Q&A: 72 Practical Answers to Your Most Pressing Questions* by Jim Grant, Bob Johnson, and Irv Richardson. Peterborough, NH: CSB, 1997

A. Children learn from each other; those with lower abilities stretch to learn from the gifted and high achievers; students without disabilities learn kindness, compassion, and caring from those who do; children with behavioral problems, or who lack positive discipline training at home, learn to behave from positive peer modeling.

Balance is a good thing! When selecting children for your looping classroom, make sure you balance your student population in terms of gender, race, socio-economic and social-emotional factors, and cognitive abilities. Children with special physical and cognitive needs should be included, but be careful not to overload your class with special-needs students. (The proportion of special-needs kids in your class should be the same as in the general population of your school.)

You should also consider the developmental levels of students when balancing the classroom. Make sure a range of developmental stages is represented; then be sure your curriculum plans accommodate all these different levels. It's especially important not to have too many developmentally young children in your classroom.

In the spring, you might use the visual organizer on the following page to begin your placement process. Any process of gathering input from parents should already have taken place. The teachers from grade levels that are sending and receiving students would meet to begin the process. Suggestions for using the placement grid are:

1. Have a grid for each teacher who will be receiving students.

2. Teachers sending students should write each student's name on a Post-it™ note (yellow for boys, blue for girls) and add any additional comments that might be helpful in the placement process.

3. Teachers sending students should place each student's name on the area of the grid that best reflects his or her level of social/emotional and cognitive development.

4. The grids are placed side-by-side, which allows for quick surveys for equity, balance, and potential difficulties.

Q. How do I make sure I have a balanced student population for my looping classroom?

Excerpted from *Looping Q&A: 72 Practical Answers to Your Most Pressing Questions* by Jim Grant, Bob Johnson, and Irv Richardson. Peterborough, NH: CSB, 1997

After reviewing the grids and agreeing on student placement, class lists can be made.

Teacher: _____

Grade: _____

Year: _____

	A.D.D.	Emotional Difficulties	Independent Learner	Motivated
Gifted			□	▨
Above Level	▨	□	□	□ ▨
At Level		▨	▨ □ □ ▨	□ □
Below Level	□		▨	▨
Title I		▨	□	▨
L.D.		□	□	▨

Depending on the demographics of your community, it may not be possible to balance the classroom in all respects; a community may be of predominantly one culture, or there may happen to be many children in the community with special needs. But spending time creating the best possible balance in your classroom, based on the population you have, will help you to optimize your instruction.

Excerpted from *Looping Q&A: 72 Practical Answers to Your Most Pressing Questions* by Jim Grant, Bob Johnson, and Irv Richardson. Peterborough, NH: CSB, 1997

PARENTAL INVOLVEMENT ASSESSMENT

Directions: Use this chart to help you assess, improve, and increase current parental involvement in your school.

Strategy	Happening	Not Happening	Could Happen	Not Likely
1. Parent/Teacher Partnership:				
Three-Way Conferences				
Student Contracts				
Summer Bridge (Summer Learning Activities)				
Other				
2. Home/School Partnership:				
Parent/Teacher Organization				
Volunteer Program				
Family Night				
Other				
3. Home/School Communication:				
Homework Hotline				
Newsletters				
School Web Site/Page				
Parent Handbook				
Surveys/Questionnaires				
Other				

Comments:

LOOPING SURVEY FOR PARENTS

Directions: Please circle A for Agree, D for Disagree, or U for Unsure in response to these questions about your child being with the same teacher(s) for two years.

My child enjoyed being with the same teacher(s) for two years.	A	D	U
My child enjoyed being with the same classmates for two years.	A	D	U
Starting the second year was less stressful for my child.	A	D	U
The second year was less stressful for me as a parent.	A	D	U
I had a better understanding of my child's education after two years with the same teacher(s).	A	D	U
At the beginning of the second year, my child understood what was expected of him/her.	A	D	U
The teacher(s) better understood my child's strengths and needs during the second year.	A	D	U
The summer between the two years was less stressful for my child.	A	D	U
I felt more comfortable communicating with my child's teacher(s) during the second year.	A	D	U
If I had it to do over, I would choose looping for my child.	A	D	U
I would recommend looping to other parents.	A	D	U

Comments:

ENCUESTA DE PADRES para la clase enlazada

Por favor circunda "Sí", si esté de acuerdo; "No", si no; o "I" para incierto/a al responder a estas preguntas sobre su hijo/a en una clase enlazada.

Mi hijo/a disfrutó de estar con el/la mismo/a maestro/a por 2 años.	Sí	No	I
Mi hijo/a disfrutó de estar con los mismos compañeros de clase por 2 años.	Sí	No	I
El comienzo del segundo año le dió menos estrés a mi hijo/a.	Sí	No	I
Llegué a comprender mejor la educación de mi hijo/a después de 2 años con el/la mismo/a maestro/a.	Sí	No	I
Al principio del segundo año, mi hijo/a entendió lo que se le esperaba.	Sí	No	I
Los maestros comprendieron mejor las abilidades y necesidades de mi hijo/a en el segundo año.	Sí	No	I
El verano entre los 2 años escolares pareció producir menos estrés para mi hijo/a al saber que él/ella tendría de nuevo el/la mismo/a maestro/a.	Sí	No	I
Sentí más cómodo/a comunicando con el/la maestro/a de mi hijo/a en el segundo año.	Sí	No	I
Si tuviera que hacerlo de nuevo, escogería una clase enlazada.	Sí	No	I
Recomendaría a otros padres una clase enlazada.	Sí	No	I

Comentarios:

LOOPING SURVEY FOR TEACHERS

Directions: Please circle A for Agree, D for Disagree, or U for Unsure in response to these questions about your child's experience in a looping classroom for two years.

I enjoyed working with the same group of students for two years.	A	D	U
My students enjoyed being with the same classmates for two years.	A	D	U
Starting the second year was less stressful for my students.	A	D	U
The second year was less stressful for me as a teacher.	A	D	U
I had a better understanding of each student's placement in the curriculum at the start of the second year.	A	D	U
At the beginning of the second year, the students understood the classroom rules and routines and knew what was expected of them.	A	D	U
I better understood each student's strengths and needs during the second year.	A	D	U
The summer between the two years was less stressful for the students and me.	A	D	U
I felt more comfortable communicating with my students' parents during the second year.	A	D	U
There was greater parent involvement during the second year of the looping classroom.	A	D	U
If I had it to do over, I would choose to teach in a looping classroom.	A	D	U
I would recommend looping to other teachers.	A	D	U

Comments:

References and Recommended Resources

Looping

Forsten, Char et al. *Looping Q&A: 72 Practical Answers to Your Most Pressing Questions*. Peterborough, NH: Crystal Springs Books, 1997.

—. *The Multiyear Lesson Plan Book*. Peterborough, NH: Crystal Springs Books, 1996.

Grant, Jim et al. *The Looping Handbook: Teachers and Students Progressing Together*. Peterborough, NH: Crystal Springs Books, 1996.

Hobbs, Julia Ann, and Carla Dawn Fisher. *Summer Bridge Activities™ 2nd Grade to 3rd Grade*. Salt Lake City, UT: Rainbow Publishing, Inc., 1994. (This is one of a series of books that bridge the different grade levels with summer activities.)

Multiage and Nongraded Education

Boyer, Ernest L. *The Basic School: A Community for Learning*. Princeton, NJ: The Carnegie Foundation for the Advancement of Teaching, 1995.

Cawelti, Gordon, ed. *Handbook of Research on Improving Student Achievement*. Arlington, VA: Educational Research Service, 1995.

Fogarty, Robin, ed. *The Multiage Classroom: A Collection*. Palatine, IL: Skylight Publishing, 1993.

—. *Think About...Multiage Classrooms: An Anthology of Essays*. Palatine, IL: Skylight Publishing, 1995.

Gaustad, Joan. "Making the Transition from Graded to Nongraded Primary Education." *Oregon School Study Council Bulletin,* vol. 35, no. 8 (April 1992).

—. "Nongraded Education: Overcoming Obstacles to Implementing the Multiage Classroom." *Oregon School Study Council Bulletin*, vol. 38, nos. 3–4 (November and December 1994).

Goodlad, John I., and Robert H. Anderson. *The Nongraded Elementary School*. New York: Teachers College Press, 1987.

Grant, Jim, and Bob Johnson. *A Common Sense Guide to Multiage Practices*. Columbus, OH: Teachers' Publishing Group, 1995.

—. Multiage *Q&A: 101 Practical Answers to Your Most Pressing Questions*. Peterborough, NH: Crystal Springs Books, 1995.

—. *Our Best Advice: The Multiage Problem Solving Handbook*. Peterborough, NH: Crystal Springs Books, 1996.

—. *The Multiage Handbook: A Comprehensive Resource for Multiage Practices*. Peterborough, NH: The Society For Developmental Education, 1996.

Miller, Bruce A. *Children at the Center: Implementing the Multiage Classroom*. Portland, OR: Northwest Regional Educational Laboratory, 1994.

Multiyear Assignment of Teachers to Students. Arlington, VA: Educational Research Service, 1997. (Information Folio)

National Education Association. *Multi-age Classrooms*. West Haven, CT: NEA Teacher-to-Teacher Books, 1995.

Rathbone, Charles et al. *Multiage Portraits: Teaching and Learning in Mixed-age Classrooms*. Peterborough, NH: Crystal Springs Books, 1993.

Virginia Education Association and Appalachia Educational Laboratory. *Teaching Combined Grade Classes: Real Problems and Promising Practices*. Charleston, WV: Appalachian Educational Laboratory, 1990.

School Change Process and Reform

Bridges, William. *Managing Transitions: Making the Most of Change*. Reading, MA: Addison-Wesley Publishing Company, 1991.

Conner, Daryl R. *Managing at the Speed of Change*. New York: Villard Books, 1995.

Fullan, Michael. *Change Forces: Probing the Depths of Educational Reform*. Bristol, PA: The Falmer Press, 1993.

Hunter, Madeline. *How to Change to a Nongraded School*. Alexandria, VA: Association for Supervision and Curriculum Development, 1992.

Prince, Julian D. *Invisible Forces: School Reform Versus School Culture*. Bloomington, IN: Phi Delta Kappa, 1989.

Saxl, Ellen R. *Assisting Change in Education: A Training Program for School Improvement Facilitators*. Alexandria, VA: Association for Supervision and Curriculum Development, 1990. (Trainer and Participant Manuals)

Evaluation Resources

Beyer, Barry K. *How to Conduct a Formative Evaluation*. Alexandria, VA: Association for Supervision and Curriculum Development, 1995.

Calhoun, Emily F. *How to Use Action Research in the Self-Renewing School*. Alexandria, VA: Association for Supervision and Curriculum Development, 1994.

Forsten, Char, Jim Grant, and Irv Richardson. *The Multiage Evaluation Book*. Peterborough, NH: Crystal Springs Books, 1999.

Sagor, Richard. *How to Conduct Collaborative Action Research*. Alexandria, VA: Association for Supervision and Curriculum Development, 1992.

Schmoker, Mike. *Results: The Key to Continuous School Improvement*. Alexandria, VA: Association for Supervision and Curriculum Development, 1996.

Teaching, Management, and Assessment in the Classroom

Albert, Linda. *A Teacher's Guide to Cooperative Discipline*. Circle Pines, MN: American Guidance Services, 1989.

Armstrong, Thomas. *Multiple Intelligences in the Classroom*. Alexandria, VA: Association for Supervision and Curriculum Development, 1994.

Caine, Renate Nummela, and Geoffrey Caine. *Making Connections: Teaching and the Human Brain*. Alexandria, VA: Association for Supervision and Curriculum Development, 1991.

Campbell, Bruce. *The Multiple Intelligences Handbook*. Stanwood, WA: Campbell and Associates, 1994.

Cirriarellie, Joellyn Thrall, ed. *Parent Letters for the Primary Grades*. Cypress, CA: Creative Teaching Press, 1997.

Clemmons, Joan et al. *Portfolios in the Classroom: A Teacher's Sourcebook*. New York: Scholastic Professional Books, 1993.

Cummings, Carol, Ph.D. *Managing to Teach: A Guide to Classroom Management*. 2d ed. Edmonds, WA: Teaching, Inc., 1996.

Davies, Anne, Colleen Politano, and Caren Cameron. *Making Themes Work*. Winnipeg, Manitoba, Canada: Peguis Publishers, 1993.

Davies, Anne et al. *Together Is Better: Collaborative Assessment, Evaluation, and Reporting.* Winnipeg, Manitoba, Canada: Peguis Publishers, 1992.

Ellis, Susan S., and Susan Whalen. *Cooperative Learning: Getting Started.* New York: Scholastic Professional Books, 1990.

Faculty, New City School. *Celebrating Multiple Intelligences: Teaching for Success.* St. Louis, MO: The New City School, Inc., 1994.

Feldman, Jean R. *Wonderful Rooms Where Children Can Bloom.* Peterborough, NH: Crystal Springs Books, 1997.

Goodman, Gretchen. *I Can Learn! Strategies and Activities for Gray-Area Children.* Peterborough, NH: Crystal Springs Books, 1995.

—. *More I Can Learn!* Peterborough, NH: Crystal Springs Books, 1997.

Grant, Jim, and Irv Richardson. *The Retention/Promotion Checklist.* Peterborough, NH: Crystal Springs Books, 1998.

Hall, Karen P., ed. *Parent Letters for the Intermediate Grades.* Cypress, CA: Creative Teaching Press, 1997.

Ingraham, Phoebe Bell. *Creating and Managing Learning Centers: A Thematic Approach.* Peterborough, NH: Crystal Springs Books, 1997.

Johnson, David, Roger Johnson, and Edythe Johnson Holubec. *Cooperative Learning in the Classroom.* Alexandria, VA: Association for Supervision and Curriculum Development, 1994.

—. *The New Circles of Learning: Cooperation in the Classroom and School.* Alexandria, VA: Association for Supervision and Curriculum Development, 1994.

Kaufeldt, Martha. *Begin With The Brain.* Tucson, AZ: Zephr Press, 1999.

Lazear, David. *Multiple Intelligence Approaches to Assessment: Solving the Assessment Conundrum.* Palatine, IL: IRI/Skylight Publishing, Inc., 1994.

—. *Seven Ways of Teaching.* Palatine, IL: IRI/Skylight Publishing, 1991.

Opitz, Michael F. *Flexible Grouping in Reading.* New York: Scholastic, Inc., 1998.

Pavelka, Patricia. *Create Independent Learners: Teacher-Tested Strategies for All Ability Levels.* Peterborough, NH: Crystal Springs Books, 1999.

Slavin, Robert. *Cooperative Learning.* Boston: Allyn and Bacon, 1995.

Sylwester, Robert. *A Celebration of Neurons: An Educator's Guide to the Human Brain*. Alexandria, VA: Association for Supervision and Curriculum Development, 1995.

Tomlinson, Carol Ann. *How to Differentiate Instruction in Mixed-Ability Classrooms*. Alexandria, VA: Association for Supervision and Curriculum Development, 1995.

Wong, Harry K., and Rosemary T. Wong. *The First Days of School: How to Be an Effective Teacher*. Mountain View, CA: Harry K. Wong Publications, Inc., 1998.

Other Professional Books of Interest to Looping Educators

Berk, Laura E., and Adam Winsler. Scaffolding *Children's Learning: Vygotsky and Early Childhood Education*. Washington, DC: National Association for the Education of Young Children, 1995.

Gardner, Howard. *Frames of Mind: The Theory of Multiple Intelligences*. 10th ed. New York: Basic Books, 1993.

—. *Multiple Intelligences: The Theory in Practice*. New York: Basic Books, 1990.

Grant, Jim. *Developmental Education in an Era of High Standards*. Rosemont, NJ: Modern Learning Press, 1998.

Healy, Jane M. *Endangered Minds*. New York: Touchstone, 1990.

—. *Your Child's Growing Mind: A Guide to Learning and Brain Development from Birth to Adolescence*. New York: Doubleday, 1987.

Kotulak, Ronald. *Inside the Brain*. Kansas City, MO: Andrews McMeel Publishing, 1996.

Members, National Education Commission on Time and Learning. *Prisoners of Time*. Washington, DC: National Education Commission on Time and Learning, 1994.

Wood, Chip. *Yardsticks: Children in the Classroom Ages 4-14; A Resource for Parents*. Greenfield, MA: Northeast Foundation for Children, 1997.

Study Kits

Forsten, Char et al. *Multiage Classrooms*. Alexandria, VA: Association for Supervision and Curriculum Development, 1996. (ASCD Professional Inquiry Kit)

Audio-Visual Resources

The Looping Video with Char Forsten and Jim Grant. Peterborough, NH: Crystal Springs Books, 1998. (Video)

Pavelka, Pat. *Using Themes and Centers to Enhance Instruction.* Peterborough, NH: Crystal Springs Books, 1997. (Video)

Web Sites for Educators and Parents

ERIC: Clearinghouse on Elementary and Early Childhood Education
http://ericps.ed.uiuc.edu/

North Dakota ICICLE Project (Internet Comprehensive Instructional and Curricular Resources for Educators): Comprehensive library of "reviewed" K–12 curriculum and instructional materials available on the Internet, which is organized by subject area, and includes links to most K–12-related news groups.
http://calvin.cc.ndsu.nodak.edu/wayne/icicle.index.html

teachernet: includes a bulletin board for multiage teachers.
www.teachernet.com

teachnet: a great site for all teachers, including multiage educators.
www.teachnet.com

Yahoo Education Resources: Includes sections on educational theory and methods, K–12 resources, math and science education, and special education.
http://www.yahoo.com/Education/

Parent Resources

National Parent Information Network
http://www.ed.gov/pubs/parents.html
http://ericps.uiuc.edu/npin/

National Parent Teacher Association
www.pta.org

School Visitations or Classroom Observations

To find out where you can visit a looping classroom or school near you, consider one of these contacts:

1. State Department of Education
2. Internet (See Web sites on p. 82.)
3. College or university with teacher education programs
4. National Alliance of Multiage Educators (N.A.M.E.; 10 Sharon Rd., P.O. Box 577, Peterborough, NH 03458; 603-924-9256; www.socdeved.com)

Sources of Data and Information

To help in your evaluation plan, consider these potential sources of data:

Existing School Sources:
1. Standardized test data
2. Student records
3. Student portfolios
4. Retention records
5. Referrals for discipline
6. Attendance records
7. Special-education referrals
8. Chapter I referrals

Questioning the Participants:
1. Interviews
2. Surveys
3. Questionnaires

Other Sources of Information:
1. Observations
2. Journals
3. Performances
4. Checklists
5. Videotapes
6. Work samples

Professional Journals as Sources of Information

Association for Supervision and Curriculum Development—*Educational Leadership*

Education Week

Harvard Newsletter

NAESP—*Principal*

Phi Delta Kappan

The School Administrator

Resources for Parental Involvement

1. Baskwill, Jane. *Parents and Teachers: Partners in Learning.* Toronto, Ontario, Canada: Scholastic, 1990.

2. Davies, Anne et al. *Together Is Better.* Winnipeg, Manitoba, Canada: Peguis Publishers, 1992. (Comprehensive book on three-way conferences among students, teachers, and parents.)

3. Ohle, Nancy, and Lakin Morely. *How to Involve Parents in a Multicultural School.* Alexandria, VA: ASCD, 1996.

4. Stenmark, Jean Kerr et al. *Family Math.* Lawrence Hall of Science, University of California, 1986. (Terrific ideas for "family math night" activities at school.)

Web Sites:

The PTA
http://www.pta.org

Great site for parents and teachers wanting methods of working with parents. Contains lots of information on how parents can help their children learn.

U.S. Department of Education
http://www.ed.gov/pubs/pubdb.html

A database of U.S. Department of Education publications in ERIC. Offers great ideas for ways schools and parents can work together.

"When I leave, I am going to really, really miss Mrs. Markon and my classmates. If you ever get Mrs. Markon, you are very lucky, because she is the best teacher. I bet I love Mrs. Markon better than anybody else will ever!"

—Jessica, 8 years old
New York

BIBLIO-INDEX

This chart directs you to books that address specific looping topics and practices identified in each column heading. The book is written for all levels except where noted. For a comprehensive list of recommended books and materials, see the reference section.

	Terms & Definitions	Advantages	Disadvantages	Student-Selection Process	Sharing Materials/ Suggestions	Changing Classroom Decision	Parental Questions/ Involvement	Management & Discipline	Learning Centers	Assessment	Flexible Grouping
Looping Q&A (Forsten et al, 1997)	4	4	4	4	4	4	4				
The Looping Handbook (Grant et al, 1996)	4	4	4		4		4	4			
The Looping Video (Jim Grant & Char Forsten)	4	4	4		4	4	4				
Multiage Handbook (Grant et al, 1996)		4	4								
Managing to Teach (Cummings, 1996)								4	4		
Begin With The Brain (Kaufeldt, 1999)											
Create Independent Learners (Pavelka, 1999)											
Creating & Managing Learning Centers (Ingraham, 1997) (Primary)									4	4	4
A Teacher's Guide to Cooperative Discipline (Albert, 1989)								4			4
Wonderful Rooms Where Children Can Bloom (Feldman, 1997) (Primary)									4	4	
The First Days of School: How to Be an Effective Teacher (Wong, 1998)								4	4	4	4